All Creation Waits

The Advent Mystery of New Beginnings

All Creation Waits

The Advent Mystery of New Beginnings

GAYLE BOSS • ILLUSTRATED BY DAVID G. KLEIN

PARACLETE PRESS

BREWSTER, MASSACHUSETTS

2018 Third Printing
2017 Second Printing
2016 First Printing

All Creation Waits: The Advent Mystery of New Beginnings

ISBN 978-1-61261-785-5

Library of Congress Cataloging-in-Publication Data

Names: Boss, Gayle, author.
Title: All creation waits : the Advent mystery of new beginnings / Gayle Boss
; illustrated by David G. Klein.
Description: Brewster MA : Paraclete Press Inc., 2016.
Identifiers: LCCN 2016026453 | ISBN 9781612617855 (trade paper)
Subjects: LCSH: Advent--Meditations. | Creation--Meditations.
Classification: LCC BV40 .B675 2016 | DDC 242/.33--dc23
LC record available at https://lccn.loc.gov/2016026453

10 9 8 7 6 5 4 3

Published by Paraclete Press
Brewster, Massachusetts
www.paracletepress.com

Printed in Canada

For Doug, and Kai and Cotter
my "grace heaped upon grace"

and for Cheryl
godmother and soul friend

CONTENTS

INTRODUCTION

*Every single creature is full of God and is a book about God.
Every creature is a word of God. If I spend enough time with
the tiniest creature, even a caterpillar, I would never have to
prepare a sermon. So full of God is every creature.*

—Meister Eckhart

When our first son was a toddler I wanted to add an Advent calendar to our family's Advent practices. Before his birth we had already begun to take back late November and December from "the holiday season," doing a few things that, though very simple, startled family and friends. We'd given up colored lights and Christmas decorations for four candles on an Advent wreath, only putting the decorations up, with the tree, on Christmas Eve. We waited until then, too, to sing or play or listen to Christmas carols, keeping quiet except to sing "O Come, O Come Emmanuel" each evening around the lit wreath. Now and then someone dared to ask us why our home was so un-Christmasy. More people asked more pointedly after our son was born—as if we were denying him some essential of childhood.

We decided to strip down and step back after I read a few paragraphs in a rather dry tome on the history of Christian liturgy. Those paragraphs worked in me like fingers lining up the cylinders of a lock. I still remember the *click* when that internal lock popped open.

I learned that the roots of Advent run deep beneath the Christian church—in the earth and its seasons. Late autumn, in the northern hemisphere, brings the end of the growing season. When early agricultural peoples had harvested their crops and stacked food in their larders, they gave a collective sigh of relief. Their long days in the fields were over. For their labor they had heaps of fruits, vegetables, grains, and meat. The group body called out, *Feast!*

At the same time, no matter how glad the party, they couldn't keep from glancing at the sky. Their growing season was over because the sun had retreated too far south to keep the crops alive. Each day throughout the fall they watched the light dwindle, felt the warmth weaken. It made them anxious, edgy. Their fires were no substitute for the sun. When they had eaten up the crop they were feasting on, how would another crop grow? Throughout December, as the sun sank and sank to its lowest point on their horizon, they felt the shadow of primal fear—fear for survival—crouching over them. They were feasting, and they were fearful, both. Yes, last year the sun had returned to their sky. But what if, this year, it didn't? Despite their collective memory, people wedded, bodily, to the earth couldn't help asking the question. Their bodies, in the present tense, asked the question.

Our bodies still ask that question. In December the dark and cold deepen, and our rational minds dismiss it as nothing. We *know* that on December 21, the winter solstice, the sun will begin its return to our sky. But our animal bodies react with dis-ease. We feel, *The light—life—is going*. Those particularly afflicted know themselves as SAD—Seasonal Affective Disorder—sufferers. Some of us cope by seizing distractions the marketplace gleefully offers: shopping, parties, more shopping.

To be sure, some part of "the holiday season" is celebration of the harvest, for us, as it was for our ancestors, even if our personal harvest doesn't involve crops and barns. We throw a party to mark the end of another year and all it's brought. We do this in a big, bright, loud way. But for us also, as for our ancestors, the dark end of the year brings unrest. It is an end. It comes without our asking and makes plain how little of life's course we control. This uncertainty, we don't know how to mark. And so it marks us. We feel weighted, gloomy even, and we feel guilty because voices everywhere in myriad ways sing out, "It's the Most Wonderful Time of the Year."

The church history book that got hold of me told me that my own annual December sadness was no reason for guilt. It was a sign of being wide awake in the world, awake enough to sense loss. And furthermore, there was a way to engage that sadness. That way was Advent.

The early Fathers of the Christian church read the ebbing of light and heat and vegetable life each year as a foreshadowing of the time when life as we know it will end completely. That it will end is the rock-bottom truth we sense deep in our primal bones every December, and it rightly terrifies us. To their and our abiding fear of a dark ending, the church spoke of an *adventus*: a coming. Faith proclaimed, *When life as we know it goes, this year and at the end of all years, One comes, and comes bringing a new beginning.*

Advent, to the Church Fathers, was the right naming of the season when light and life are fading. They urged the faithful to set aside four weeks to fast, give, and pray—all ways to strip down, to let the bared soul recall what it knows beneath its fear of the dark, to know what Jesus called "the one thing necessary": that there is One who is the source of all life, One who comes to be with us and in us, even, especially, in darkness and death. One who brings a new beginning.

———✦———

This is Christian tradition at its best, moving in step with creation. When the sun's light and heat wane, the natural world lets lushness fall away. It strips down. All energy is directed to the essentials that ensure survival. Engaging in Advent's stripping practices—fasting, giving away, praying—we tune into the rhythms humming in the cells of all creatures living in the northern hemisphere. We tune into our own essential rhythms.

So when I wanted to add an Advent calendar to our practice, I looked for one that would, like fasting, giving away, and praying, help us enjoin earth's seasonal rhythm. The ones at Christian bookstores featured a thumbnail-sized cast of the Nativity behind the daily doors. Better than pictures of candy canes and gift packages. But I was looking for daily miniatures that were less about Christ's human birth and more about the *need* for that birth. I wanted my little boy, opening each door, to sense that Advent is about darkness—and hope, fear—and hope, loss—and hope.

Pregnant with my second child, I set about making an Advent calendar. The pictures I found myself drawing behind the little cut-out doors were of creatures. Behind door number one, a turtle at the bottom of a pond. Behind door number two, a diamond-skinned snake. Then a loon, a wild goose, a bear, a doe, a crow . . . As a companion to the calendar I made a little book. Each December day after Kai opened a door, I read a bit of a poem or song or natural history that linked the creature behind that door to the heart of Advent: "Turtle is buried now in mud at the bottom of the pond. Encased in darkness, she is utterly still. She waits. . . ."

I drew a turtle behind the door of December 1 because, days before, my son's godmother had sent me her meditation on turtle as a symbol of the soul in its dark season. And because I knew my son, like all children, liked pictures of animals.

That was more than twenty Advents ago. Both boys still come home some days in Advent. We still open a calendar door and read about the animal for that day. They still want me to ask the only question I've ever asked at the end of the reading: *Why do we have a turtle on our Advent calendar? Why a bear? Why a loon?*

Looking at the animal portraits year after year shows us how a healthy soul responds to encroaching darkness. And there's more than one response. There's the turtle response, the loon response, black bear's response. . . . When that primal fear of the dark—of the end—begins to slide over us, animals unselfconsciously and forthrightly offer unfearful responses. They take in the threat of dark and cold, and they adapt in amazing and ingenious ways. They shape themselves to life as it is given.

Some of the animal portraits here are elaborations of ones on our family Advent calendar. Others are of animals I've come to know since making it. All twenty-four enact heart and soul realities for us. Each in its way says: *The dark is not an end, but a door. This is the way a new beginning comes.*

The practice of Advent has always been about helping us to grasp the mystery of a new beginning out of what looks like death. Other-than-human creatures—sprung, like us, from the Source of Life—manifest this mystery without question or doubt. The more I'm with animals and the more I learn about them, the more I know they can be more than our companions on this planet. They can be our guides. They can be to us "a book about God . . . a word of God," the God who comes, even in the darkest season, to bring us a new beginning.

ADVENT 1

Painted Turtle

The day is bright and warm for December 1, but the logs in the marsh pond are bare. Spring to summer into early fall they served, on sunny days, as spa to a dozen or so painted turtles. I would see them basking, splay-legged, stretching their leathery necks out full length, avid for every luscious atom of sunlight and sun-warmth.

Out of sight now, they've not escaped the harsher cold that's coming.

The water is maybe waist-deep in this pond, but a murky soup, clogged with roots and plants. One day in the fall, as water and air cooled, at some precise temperature an ancient bell sounded in the turtle brain. A signal: *Take a deep breath*. Each creature slipped off her log and swam for the warmer muck bottom. Stroking her way through the woven walls of plant stems, she found her bottom place. She closed her eyes and dug into the mud. She buried herself.

And then, pulled into her shell, encased in darkness, she settled into a deep stillness. Her heart slowed—and slowed—almost to stopping. Her body temperature dropped—and stopped just short of freezing. Now, beneath a layer of mud, beneath the weight of frigid water and its skin of ice and skim of snow, everything in her has gone so still she doesn't need to breathe. And anyway, the iced-over pond will soon be empty of oxygen. Sunk in its bottom-mud, for six months she will not draw air into her lungs. To survive a cold that would kill her, or slow her so that predators would kill her, she slows herself beyond breath in a place where breath is not possible.

And waits. As ice locks in the marsh water and howling squalls batter its reeds and brush, beneath it all she waits. It is her one work, and it is not easy. Oxygen depletion stresses every particle of her. Lactic acid pools in her bloodstream. Her muscles begin to burn—her heart muscle, too, a deadly sign. That acid has to be neutralized, and calcium is the element to do it. Out of her bones, then out of her shell, her body pulls calcium, slowly dissolving her structure, her shape, her strength. But to move to escape—requiring breath—in a place where there is no oxygen—that would suffocate her. So, though she is dissolving, every stressed particle of her stays focused on the silver bead of utter quietude.

It's this radical simplicity that will save her. And deep within it, at the heart of her stillness, something she has no need to name, but something we might call trust: that one day, yes, the world will warm again, and with it, her life.

Muskrat

Sitting up and hunched forward like a precision jeweler, the muskrat guides the tender stem end of a cattail into his mouth, long-clawed front paws holding, peeling, chewing, all at the same time, fast and ravenous. When he gets to the tough part, he tosses it aside, takes another from his pile, and bites.

I admired him a long time on a brilliant early morning last summer at the edge of the pond, admired his voracious yet meticulous eating—eating with a purpose. That purpose, I first supposed, was to pack away as many calories as possible and live off fat reserves when the cattails age into brown husks, when ice seals up the pond, and when the dimly lit days invite a long nap.

But muskrat is no winter napper. He's apt to be swimming under the ice cap this very minute, his tail—flattened vertically, like a belt on edge—propelling him just as swiftly and deftly as in summer, thanks to an ingenious recalibration of body chemistry that enables his blood to carry and his muscles to store more oxygen in winter. Flesh and blood rich in oxygen, wrapped in a luxuriant double-layered fur coat that traps an insulating air pocket next to his skin and repels water from without, he is an avid frigid-water swimmer. As he needs to be.

Unlike his cousin the northern beaver, he has stored no food for winter. But his busy metabolism every day drives him to eat the equivalent of a third of his body weight in fresh vegetation. So today and every winter day he has no choice but to dive beneath the ice for the plants that still grow on the bottomlands.

Able-bodied as he is for this, the icy water rapidly saps his heat and strength. He has to surface in the middle of the pond to warm up. So from beneath the ice he's built a refuge—a push-up, it's called—by pushing sticks and stalks up through cracks in the ice into a heap, a mound. He pushes his body up into the mounded shelter, shakes his fur dry and shivers to raise his body temperature. He allows others to join him—even non-kin—for the precious extra heat of a group huddle. If he feels too weak to dive, he may eat some of his shelter from the inside—though always with an eye on the walls' thickness; he can't risk opening it to the winter wind.

It's a little breathing room, this heap of sticks on the pond ice. A dark little room, like his dark little den dug into the pond bank. Retreating to his dark rooms to rest and breathe—sometimes alone, often with others—this is how he survives the months of cold that can stop his plucky, industrious heart. Warmed, invigorated there, with a flick of his tail he dives sleek and quick to the very bottom, where fresh food always grows.

Black Bear

Walking the northern Michigan hardwoods where I was raised, restless, I make myself stand still. Somewhere in these eight hundred acres a black bear is sunk in sleep. A month ago already, beneath some fallen tree or stump, she dug a den rounded to the curl of her body. She raked bits of bark and grass over its floor and eased herself in. I crouch, close my eyes, and imagine that ball of furred muscle lax and loose somewhere nearby.

For weeks before she lay herself down, her whole self had been shifting, making ready for another life. Late in summer, just when most berries and nuts ripen, she grew ravenous. Seven, eight hours a day she camped in wild raspberry, blackberry, gooseberry, and huckleberry patches, pawing and licking fruit into her mouth, then, to rest, dropping to her belly and breathing in the fallen gems. Cloyed of sweet, she sniffed out savory—jewelweed, swamp thistle, cattail, and saxifrage—snacking on yellow jackets, ants, and beetle larvae along the way, finishing the day in a grove of beechnuts or hazelnuts or hickory nuts—tripling, even quadrupling her usual day's calorie intake. Still the trustworthy voice inside her urged, *Eat, eat more!*

Lush, warm, the Indian summer days were lost on her. Her gaze was fixed ahead, her every move food-purposed, her intention fierce and singular. Until the voice prompted an utter turnaround. *Let go*, it said. *Go limp*.

The nut trees and berry bushes are skeletons now. Crouched in the snow-muffled quiet I imagine hearing her slow breathing. I imagine smelling slow-burning bear—the fat she made from all those nuts, berries, bugs, and plants melting and fueling her sleep. She is shrinking—except in the den deep inside her body. There she is multiplying, balls of cells swelling into new forms of her.

Maybe she dreams of the life growing inside her. Did she foresee it all the while she ate and grew, ate and grew? Did she perceive it when she lay down? Whatever hints—or none—she had of its purpose, she knew absolutely a compelling urge. She obeyed that urge, and now, in its own time, while she sleeps, it takes shape. Two shapes.

About eight weeks from now, while she still sleeps, the cubs will tumble out of her. Ten ounces each and blind, they'll find her nipples and set straight to nursing. While she sleeps, they'll nurse and grow, nurse and grow, their hunger draining her body's stores.

In late March, when the air warms, she'll wake slowly. Imagine the moment when, spent and thin, she finds four bright eyes looking back at her.

Chickadee

Nearly every winter day the small flock would arrive a-flurry at the feeder outside the window of Miss Milner's second-grade classroom. "Chick-a-dee-dee-dee," she would sing. "Chick-a-dee-dee-dee," we would answer.

Small round bodies with large round heads capped in black, they were acrobats, twirling upside down on the feeder and on the pine boughs brushing it. They didn't fly away when I pressed my nose to the windowpane but looked me in the eye, I was sure, and peeped.

Perhaps she was sparing us—children who still felt the suffering of creatures—but Miss Milner didn't tell us that every cold night those cheery birds walked a tightrope between life and death to greet us the next morning. Half-an-ounce of feather, flesh, and hollow bone, a chickadee in your palm would feel like the weight of two nickels. Like any living thing lightweight relative to its length and width, it loses heat quickly. So the little bird must eat continually during winter's short daylight hours to stoke its metabolic fires for the long night to come. Even so, on a below-zero night the fires can go out. Even tucked into the shelter of a tree hole, even with the ability to drop its body temperature substantially to

save energy, a chickadee on a winter night burns through all the calories it ate during the day. Before dawn, as soon as there's light enough to see, the chickadee flutters out, famished, its tiny brain intent on seeds.

Tiny, its brain, but bigger now, in Advent, than in spring.

I tip my head at the chickadee tipping his head quizzically at me. Inside that black skullcap his hippocampus is bulged with a precise map of his half-mile territory, an X marking each flap of tree bark or log crack where he's stashed a seed. Since late summer his brain's memory center has been growing, adding neurons to record the location of every single cached seed—thousands of them. As he eats them up through the rest of winter, the map and his hippocampus will shrink. Will the seed map be gone before the ice and snow?

No wonder the chickadees at Miss Milner's feeder seemed ecstatic. Their winter stashes would last longer thanks to the bonanza—best, the black-oil sunflower seeds—she poured out every morning.

As they swirl and twirl and hop and flit about my feeder now, they seem a flock of St. Francises. Like the saint wed to Lady Poverty, every winter day the equation of their existence is open: Will there be enough of what they need to take them through the dark night, into tomorrow? Beyond reason, like the saint, they act as if the question is truly an opening, a freedom, a joy.

Whitetail Deer

Gliding through the woods in groups of two, three, or four, their coats the color of brush and bark render them nearly invisible to us. So when, in October, we see herds of them out in the open, it seems a curtain has been pulled back on a secret society. They know the cold is coming. Banding together against predators, they forage widely in the fields before their food freezes, or vanishes under snow.

But then, a drive deeper than feeding seizes them. By November both bucks and does, restless, verge on reckless. Trumping food and wariness, the primal urge to reproduce one's self and one's kind surges with the winds of the coming, killing cold. "The rut" it's called, from a Latin word for "roar," and in the part of Michigan where I live it crescendos in the first days of Advent.

Bucks set out now as solitary travelers, ranging their claimed territory and marking it profusely. An area's strongest buck has won the right in early fall sparring matches to mark most, advertising his virility. He rubs his antlers against soft-bark saplings—though fence posts will do—and in the rubbing, glands on his forehead seep his distinctive scent onto the gouged wood.

He paws the ground duff, too, clearing a circle in which he urinates, leaving his news. Then, on a slight branch at head height—he's chosen the place with an eye to this branch—he thrashes his antlers or bites to break the tip. Gently, eyes closed, he rubs the freshened end along the side of his face, back and forth across sensitive spots that coat the stem tip with his scent.

He has created a multi-sensory surround. Coming to it, does recognize a mate that will give them strong fawns. They seek him. He chases them. When he is elsewhere, other bucks intercept the does he's after. In the twenty-four-hour window when a doe will mate, she and the buck of the moment enact a ritual of motion, touch, sound, and scent before coming together.

This vigorous, elaborate dance engrosses whitetail deer in early Advent. They rest briefly, eat little, move, move, move, driven to re-create themselves.

Then it's over. By the end of December the more commanding cold reins in their roaring blood. They regroup—bucks together, does together—and, before deep snow hobbles them, follow memory's thread to white cedar swamps, where the boughs' dense weave shelters them from wind, from snow, from dogs and wolves. They have done with all their might what they can to continue themselves. Now they lie down together, sharing warmth, little more than their fat stores to feed them.

Huddled together, they are more hidden from us now than in any other season. If two or three should materialize, still as stone among the trees, it seems a vision. Soon, they vanish, slipping back to the cedar swamp to wait as the cold deepens and fawns grow in the does' bellies.

Honey Bee

The snow doesn't yet cover the foot of my boot, so the walking's still easy among the hardwoods. I have my dog with me as a hearing aid. When I find a hollow oak tree I call her and watch as she sniffs around it, hoping to see her stop and cock her head and stare intently at the trunk. If it were summer and if they were here, we both could hear the hum. Now, if they're here, I'm not sure even her smart, sharp ears could pick it up. What's the sound of twenty thousand honey bees shivering?

If they're here—all females in a winter hive—they're clustered together inside, queen at the heart of their sisterhood. The fine, transparent wings they beat hard in summer's heat—a constant buzzing fan to keep the hive from cooking—they hold, now, folded and still. The tiny muscles to which those wings are attached shiver. One honey bee shivering her flight muscles does not make much heat. But twenty thousand, huddled together, shivering, can keep the queen and the colony's honey supply at their core at a tropical ninety-two degrees Fahrenheit, even as blizzard winds, inches away, flail the trunk.

This calls for carefully timed choreography. When the bees on the outside layer of the cluster feel their body temperature fall to near forty-two degrees

Fahrenheit—a cold that would paralyze them—they push inward toward the radiant center. The next outermost layer takes their sisters' place, backs to the cold. From edge to center, center to edge, inward and outward they move, one hypnotic, looping dance.

At the heart of the dance lies the queen. She is every bee's reason for being. Without a queen the colony would fall into chaos. Nurse bees, grooming her, pass her scent back through the ranks. It tells all the news of her health, which is their health. They smell that now, in Advent, she's laying no eggs. There is no brood to feed. Each bee senses that her one obligation is to give the smallest motion of her flight muscles to the collective work of keeping the queen and the colony's honey stores warm. The whole hive knows they will survive only if they shiver together.

Some of them in the shivering cluster will die of old age. Had they hatched in the flowering season, their labor for the hive's survival—harvesting nectar and pollen from as many as two thousand flowers a day—would have killed them in four weeks or less, their wings worn to nubbins. But hatched on the cusp of winter they may live six months. They will know only the dark hive, the press of their sisters' bodies. They will never fly, never fall into a flower. They give their lives to shivering together in the dark, the tiny repetitive gestures of each, added together, a music beyond our hearing, sustaining a future for the community.

Chipmunk

In the sheltered south corner of my doorway where the sun has kissed away the snow I hear a *chirp-chirp-chirp-chirp*, pointed as a metronome. Ticking items off some list, a chipmunk sits up tall on the warming cement slab. I try, peanut offering in hand, to ease the latch open soundlessly, but the chipmunk jerks, spins, and vanishes down his hole.

The cement slab is sinking on the side fronting the door, thanks to this burrower. His tunnelworks clearly start at my door, but who can tell where they go from there? With forefeet half the size of paperclips, he's dug down maybe four or five times the length of his body and out as far as a two-story house is tall—though not that straight. Up in the wide bright world this morning, he's taking what's apt to be his last sunbath for a while. Winter is about to settle in its cold bulk for a three-month stay, banishing the chipmunk to his basement. Unlike his cousins, squirrels at home in the trees, he would freeze above ground. Even in the insulated earth he survives only by careful calculation.

Compulsively all fall he packed his cheek pouches with nuts and seeds and sped to rooms he'd hollowed out along the sides of his tunnel—pantries holding

altogether up to a bushel of winter provisions. He keeps inventory, working for variety. If one sort of seed spoils, he wants plenty of other sorts. Such a well stocked pantry, though, is a magnet for thieves in the beneath, and so above ground he's stored more reserves, hiding them from hungry thieves there, too.

He will keep up his gathering, storing, inventorying—above ground, below ground, relentless, never sure of enough—until, finally, the cold says: *Stop. Or die.* Then he'll slip down through his tunnel to a leaf-lined sleeping chamber and ball up. His restless heart slows from 350 beats per minute to fifteen. He barely breathes. His body cools.

If a weasel should find him so, he will be dead before he knows what bit him. Awake, he can likely escape. So he sleeps in snatches—a few days, a couple of weeks—pulling himself up out of torpor to inspect the tunnel, the exits, the pantries, and to eat. If provisions seem low, he might pick a warm day and pop up briefly to raid a bird feeder or find one of his above-ground stashes. Which means risking a hawk or cat watching for dark stripes against snow. So he considers staying put and saving food by sleeping a longer stretch. But that gives the weasel better odds. Also, he has to consider how long this winter might last and how to save food for spring—whenever that comes—so he'll be strong enough then to pursue a mate.

A tiny master of risk assessment, he calculates and recalculates all winter long. There's no formula, no group-think to fall back on. Flexibility is all. Each chipmunk must, for and by himself, consider which of several choices will most likely bring him through the cold dark days to the other side of winter, strong. He must do this continually, with no guarantees. Today, heart beating fast, he makes today's choice.

Cottontail

Nose pressed to the cold glass, I squint through the grainy gray dusk filling up our backyard already at five o'clock. A lump breaks from the thickening dark and hops—then again, and twice more—to a scraggly buckthorn with a few green leaves, and stretches up.

Every evening I watch for this eastern cottontail. She lives, I think, deep inside the brush pile at the edge of the narrow woods. Late summer and fall I saw her more often, and earlier, before the sun had fully set, her gray-brown coat pieced seamlessly into the pattern of tree trunks, underbrush, and weeds. She would eat—almost anything green—then pause, settling into herself, into her surroundings, tucked and compact, the picture of contemplation. Dozens of times I tried to creep close to sit with her, to soak up her peace, only to have her bolt—bursting from rest to a zigging-zagging dash in less than a heartbeat.

That lightning-bolt dash is now her one defense. Where once she blended into the ground cover, she now stands out in any light like a cork in a pool of milk. In the snow her feet leave neat pointers to her hiding place. And her many predators, who are as hungry as she, are watching.

She takes precautions. She doesn't venture out until the dusk is as dark as her coat. If snow has fallen, before she looks for twigs or bark to gnaw, she first packs down the fluff and powder on trails she's made from her door to nearby cover. Even an inch of snow bogs her bolt. Keen escape artist that she is, she keeps three or four trails, alternate routes, groomed for fast getaway.

When she's packed the trails and tested them for speed, she'll slip back into her resting place—just a shallow hollow she's scraped in the ground beneath the brush pile or a tangled thicket or the tent of a young spruce tree. She could dig a burrow, to hide underground. She's got the front feet for it. She'd be warmer there—and trapped, no space for a zigzag dash. Does a hole in the ground feel to her like a grave? She chooses instead a brushy hermitage above ground and there draws herself in, concentrating all her warmth inward.

It will be warmth enough, mostly. A few of winter's sharpest days will force her to crawl underground, into an abandoned skunk or woodchuck den. Barely in. She'll huddle near the exit, alert, waiting for the first gentling of the cold. More than the hole's warmth she wants space to leap and bound away.

In exchange for space to artfully dodge the hungers that pursue her, she must be still, very still, when she can. She must shelter herself, warm herself. She's practicing now. Beneath the buckthorn she's gathered herself, ears laid against her head, settled on the fine first snow. Utterly still, she is utterly alert. In her stillness is her leap.

Common Loon

Most days in December the northern lakes where I grew up chop and slap and slosh. But an eerie music is missing. It's as if the ancient shamans have quit their ritual chants and left the circle to the shuffles and mumbles of onlookers.

Glossy black above, white beneath, glinting in white-banded necklaces, chinstraps, and dappled robes, common loons glided on the lakes from May to October, piercing souls with their calls. The striking plumage, the calls—all, in spring and summer, is in service of offspring.

In early spring loons put on their black-and-white ritual dress to woo mates and to warn off rivals. The males rise up in the water, beating their heavy wings, yodeling, signaling, *This is my mate, my lake, my nest, my chick*, ready to press that insistence to the death. If an adversary approaches any of these, he seems to laugh, manic with alarm. If a mate or chick drifts too far, the partner or parent will wail, *Here! Come here!* Ten million years before any human heard them, loons shivered the lakes with their calls.

But by early September they prepare for another life. Surviving chicks have grown to independence. Adults, freed from the need to mate and ever defend

one's own, shed their bold identity. They let the spectacular feathers fall away, to be replaced by plain gray. Through the fall they gather and swim in peaceable flocks, former rivals and all, feeding communally. They give up their piercing calls for gentle hoots, to bond with and assure each other, *I'm here, we're here.*

Together they were gathering strength. When ice began to crackle the lake edges the adults set out on an arduous journey. Built heavy and solid-boned for deep diving, loons have to flap their stout wings continuously—250 times every minute—to stay aloft. No missing even a single beat, not for seven or eight hundred miles.

Their young were not with them. Juveniles lingered on their birth lakes and set out later, small groups of them alone, left to an inner guide to pilot them to a place they've never been.

All who were strong enough to survive the trip are floating now along the Atlantic coast. Regrouped, they're resting, regaining strength. There's yet another exertion to come—one of a different order and more threatening. In late winter the twenty-two flight feathers that carried each bird here will all drop out at once. Then, if they try to fly, they fall. They swim slowly as their bodies siphon energy into the growing of all-new flight feathers.

Their bold and brilliant summer selves have vanished. Adrift, winter loons go silent. These are not the breathtaking, thrilling birds we looked and listened for all spring and summer. These are merely gray birds bobbing on the gray ocean waves, vulnerable and small. Do they remember who they were a season ago or imagine who they might be in the next? They give no sign. They ride the waves, hushed, nearly invisible.

Wood Frog

This is the place on the trail to the pond where I very nearly stepped on him. Who could blame me? He's painted in the precise colors and patterns of the leaf litter, twigs, and weeds, made to be invisible, especially to snakes. A breath before my boot came down on him, I saw him—only because he lunged into deeper leaf cover.

That was in September. Another year's leaves layer the ground now, all of them the color of wood frogs. And over the leaves, three inches of snow. If, by X-ray vision, I could see under which single leaf the wood frog sits in the shallow bed he's dug, if I were to reach beneath his leaf-and-snow blanket, he would not leap from me. I could place him in the palm of my hand, a perfect fit, and trace the robber's mask drawn across his jaw; I could stroke the sun-yellow belly.

Because his sun has gone out. His arteries and veins are frozen canals, the spaces between his cells filled with ice crystals. His summer-supple skin has turned crunchy. His heart is silent as a stone. Not even the weakest current crackles in his brain. And he is not dead.

He is what scientists call "extreme tolerant."

Before his tolerance was put to the full test, he had a couple of weeks to practice. In late fall, when temperatures after dark first dropped below freezing, he felt the chill seep in and snake through his body, every atom of him stunned. Whatever was moist tended toward ice. But first his liver surged, sending a thick sugar syrup into his cells, plumping them, to keep them from the collapse of internal frostbite. He took fewer and fewer breaths, and then. . . .

Woke, gulping, in the next day's warmer daylight, his blood moving like a sticky river, cell walls slippery and wet again. When light and temperature dropped away again that night, a cold thumb again suspended his every animation. His world, and he in it, faded to black.

And with the morning light, came back. In and out with the light, thawing and freezing, the wood frog kept time to the quickening and cooling of air molecules.

One day he didn't wake. Though the morning air brightened, it didn't warm; it stayed the slow cold of ice. So he, tuned precisely to his milieu, stayed ice.

As he is now and shall be, until the rhythm shifts. When the air warms, he will too, if only for a day or a few during a January thaw. He'll find himself in his leaf bed, alive and well, and stretch his stiff frog legs. Then he'll let himself go as-good-as-dead again when the cold comes back, as it will.

There will come a warm day in spring when the ice goes out—of the ponds, of his blood—and doesn't return. Then with dozens of other wood frogs he'll hop to the pond and send up a thrilling chorus: *Death, we've robbed you of your ruin, we've taken you in.*

Raccoon

Walking at dawn one summer morning I watched a mother raccoon lead her two kits along the edge of a little stream. The kits dawdled. The mother chittered at them with what sounded like annoyance. She'd had them up and out since sunset, showing them where the fat blackberries and mulberries grow, how to listen for earthworms underground and dig them up, how to use their nimble fingers to turn over rocks in the stream and nab the quick crayfish beneath. Probably she was tired. Probably her belly was full. And on the path to their sleeping den the kits were lollygagging.

Every night from late spring through the fall she took them on this scavenger hunt, showing them the hundreds of things the world supplies a raccoon to eat, even French fries and chocolate cake, though enjoying these sometimes means solving the locks and lids of garbage bins. Raccoons may well be earth's most easy-to-please eaters.

When they sense the harsh season coming, they choose from their long menu foods that will add quick pounds. Their bodies deposit the new fat along their backs and bottoms. Their tails, too, become dense tubes of fat. And along with

their flesh, their fur grows thicker. All this, so that when the wind blows cold they can tuck in their heads and fold their forebodies beneath the fat blankets of their backsides, then wrap their balled selves with a heavy band of tail to become self-insulating fur bundles.

In summer the mother raccoon beds her kits down in any protected niche they find near the end of a night's trek. In winter she's more strategic. She tucks them into a snug place that will hold close any body heat escaping from their fur bundles. A tree hollow is nice. But a woodchuck den—complete with a deep-sleeping woodchuck, none the wiser—or a chimney will do. As they do with food, raccoons improvise, they adapt, they make the most of whatever a place and time present.

The stream still trickles, but no raccoon has walked through the snow beside it. Probably, the mother is inside one of the big trees nearby, curled tight, with the two smaller furball-kits rolled in close. Cousins may have joined them as extra space heaters. While temperatures lag below freezing they're content to sleep day and night, even if the cold lasts for weeks.

But they sleep no more soundly than I. A sharp rap on their tree's trunk or a dog's bark could snap them awake. Sleeping lightly, they're alert to predators, but alertness has its price: they burn through their fat blankets faster than hibernators. So when warm air wafts into their tree hollow the raccoon family rouses for a night out. On a warm night they won't burn as much fat going out to forage, and the food they find will add padding to their thinning backsides. At dark they ease headfirst down the trunk to the ground. The snow cover makes for slim pickings. But pick they will, with their clever fingers, and dig and sniff and listen, willing to take and eat whatever the cold dark world offers.

Little Brown Bat

Darting through the dark they take tight turns at top speed, drop into quick rolls, then pull up and sidestep in mid-air—maybe for fun, and surely to snatch insects humming over the evening pond. Come fall, quickly cooling air stills these lives that bats eat. The little browns feel the chill, too. Even in September, when they're heaviest, bats lose body heat faster than any other animal with a backbone. But a marathon flight to a climate where warmth and bugs are abundant would kill them. Instead they find a place where all year the temperature, while cool, is reliable to the utmost: the nearest cave or abandoned mine.

Males arrive first, then females with their pups. Scattered since April, they reunite in a great bat convention, as many as a quarter million swarming at the cave's mouth, flying in and out from sunset to sunrise for several days. It's a whirling dance of greeting, courting, and mating.

Satisfied, they fly inside, finding chambers where the temperature is a constant forty-two to forty-five degrees Fahrenheit. They flip themselves upside down, toes clutching the nubbled rock, and fold their wings, skin membranes

thinner than the thinnest-spun silk. Across the cavern dome they scooch and jostle, pressing close, knitting themselves into a glossy brown fur stole. Males and females, old and young, some of different species—the many meld into one heat-sharing body.

Even at rest, tucked within the One, little browns cannot sustain their usual inner life. Each bat must reset its normal—drastically. Together, hanging very still, they slow their resting hearts from four hundred beats per minute to twenty; they will stop breathing entirely for up to forty-eight minutes. On cold spring nights they practiced this self-preserving rest in small groups, huddling in trees or under eaves and waking when the day warmed. Now the congregation as a whole falls all the way through mere rest into deep torpor. Down sixty degrees Fahrenheit, each bat's body goes as cold as the air of the cave. Water droplets condense on their fur. They sparkle and seem dead.

And then, prompted only by some inner stoker, they can bring their body furnaces back up to flying heat in half an hour. This happens about every three weeks. A few wake—thirsty—and sip the water droplets from their fur. Their rustling wakes their next-wing neighbors, who wake their neighbors. Soon the cave is a percussive chorus. The bats fly for a few hours, flushing toxins from their tissues. Then they settle back into a furred mass and fall again through the shaft of stillness, stopping just shy of oblivion's floor.

The air of their crypt is changeless. But one day some mystery within them whispers, *Spring*. Scouts fly out to test whether it's true. They bring back the news and the rest—thin and hungry after a six-month fast—disperse on the fresh winds. But not before all their senses take note of the location. When cold threatens again they'll remember the place of their communion, and return.

Opossum

He should not be here. Not in the basement window well where he fell sometime in the night, sniffing out food. Not in Michigan, nor any other state where winter temperatures sit below freezing many days in succession. We lift the opossum, held in the clasp of two rakes. When we open those gates and he quick-waddles into the woods, I bow to him, to the wonder of his survival.

Opossums not unlike this one watched the dinosaurs die; they are that ancient. And they haven't evolved much since their tropical beginnings. The northern winter's cold will leave nearly all with scars: a missing tail-tip and ragged ears. The opossum's tail and ears, being hairless, naked, are quickly bit by frost, and bits of them fall off. This would happen less often if the animal would stay in his leaf-lined den during cold snaps. He does try. But if the cold lasts more than three or four days, hunger forces him out.

He has done his best, through summer and fall, to add body fat, eating very nearly anything, living or dead. But unlike a raccoon or skunk, when cold and snow come he can't slow his metabolism and sleep to burn that fat more slowly. In fact, his furnace works overtime, burning fat faster. And though he is more

adept than a rat or dog at remembering where he's once found food, he doesn't carry it home and cache it away.

So to add fat-fuel he must go out. Slow and uncamouflaged, he has no defenses except a menacing, toothy hiss. He can be scared to what looks like death—collapsed, unconscious, oozing a noxious green slime that may or may not put off the scarer. Of course he wants to go out when the night is darkest. But that's when the night is coldest. And the coat he wears not only leaves his tail and ears and toes exposed; it's not really a *winter* coat at all. It has no down hairs next to his skin to insulate him and no true guard hairs to repel snow or sleet. Temperatures below twenty degrees Fahrenheit will freeze him rather quickly. During a spell of nights colder than that, he may risk waiting. Or he may choose to go out for food when the sun warms the day—and shines a light on him for predators. He gambles either way. Darkness or warmth—which gives him better odds? He makes the decision alone. Shy, solitary, he dens without even the small comfort of shared warmth.

He is only here in snow-covered winters because we are. His ancestors began inching north with the pioneers. Where humans build barns, sheds, and garages, basements and attics—shelters warmer than burrows—where we grow gardens and put out garbage bins—reliable food supplies—opossums can beat the odds the cold stacks against them.

The opossum in our back woods has my neighbors and me. We're his best adaptation to winter. And he very nearly died in my window well. A naturalist tells me that, had we plucked the opossum from the well by his tail and slid a supporting hand under his back, he would not have snarled and twisted, trying to fight, break free, flee. He would have abandoned himself to our hands, one forepaw clasping the other, a posture that looks like petition, like prayer.

Wild Turkey

In summer the odds are less than fifty-fifty that I'll see them on the south-facing slope above the swamp. But in Advent, if I'm up with the sun, I'm lucky nearly every morning.

It's a short walk to the slope, and often I hear the flock before I see them. To me they sound like a litter of small puppies tussling, though naturalists hear cats and call the sound "cluck-purring." Ten hens are rowing through the hardwoods, stroking forward with long wattled necks. The males—the younger jakes and the older toms—keep their own societies, elsewhere. Here, a stone's toss away, one hen sees me and yelps! and all ten break into a run—surprisingly fast for creatures that look like inflated bellows balanced on sticks. Even supposing I could give chase and come close, they would then pop open their wide wings, hurl themselves into the treetops, and glare down at me, chucking their *putt-putt* alarm. No surprise that adult turkeys suffer no serious natural predators.

Even sub-zero cold doesn't trouble them. But snow—the accumulating kind—poses real threat. Snow covers the acorns, beechnuts, and hickory nuts—high energy foods—that they feed to their furnaces, burning hot and fast. Now the snow, still shallow, little impedes their nut hunt. They shovel it aside with their long and strong four-toed feet and gulp the uncovered nuts. Of which there are many on this slope, which is why they camp here in winter, roosting on the big oak and beech limbs above. Also, these birds know that because the slope tilts south, toward the sun, snow will melt more quickly from the grounded nuts. Shrewdly they've shrunk their usual range to a small plot—this particular plot—for a winter home.

Another reason for here: in a few weeks the snow even on this southern slope is apt to be as high as their thighs. Each day they take its measure from the treetops. Thigh deep—no plowing through. They cackle a signal to each other and sail downslope fifty yards to the swamp edge. There, seeps—patches where warmer groundwater bubbles to the surface—grow a wild salad of winter cress and ferns. While seep greens generate little heat in the turkey gut, it's what they have, here.

What they'd like is a thaw—if not enough to bare the ground, then for the refreeze that forms a walkable crust. Gingerly they test the surface. If it holds they quick-step a hundred yards or so to a wild field, eager beaks gleaning barberry, winterberry, and hawthorn bushes, always ready to hurry back to the woods before the air warms and the crust gives way, shackling them.

If the snow does not thaw, if it falls thick and blows, this place provides them one last recourse. They've seen that the swamp also has fir trees, and fir branches make sturdy canopies to roost beneath, dry and unblown. Each hen on her branch fluffs her feathers against the cold. Together, they might sit fluffed for more than a week, burning body fat, calling reassurances to each other, especially to the youngest, of slightest heft: *Together we can outlast this, right here in this sufficient place.*

Common Garter Snake

Splayed on a rock in September, he can feel summer's punch draining from the sun. Through thin, naked skin he senses heat evaporating, degree by degree, from the air—and from his body's loose S.

A week later I see him slide across the gravel path. Now the sun has become, besides his body's warmer, this garter snake's compass. He lifts his thumb-sized head skyward, seeking direction toward a remembered destination. En route, he'll look for landmarks he noted on last year's trek—this oak stump, that boulder. He'll flick his red forked tongue to collect the scent that female garters, ahead of him, effuse, assuring him, *This is the way*. He has to arrive before the temperature drops below freezing for longer than a day. If he doesn't, his lithe self will freeze stiff as a stick.

He glides along his remembered travel lane for a mile, two miles, intent on a particular hole in the ground. Without any tools for digging, this garter, like all snakes, is at the mercy of other creatures, or the mercy of the earth itself, to open

a door to the warmer underworld. He knows one door, one den that can meet his needs in the difficult season ahead. It's mapped in his mind and in the minds of all the area's garter snakes. Solitary creatures from the moment of birth, in fall they follow their maps and slither in from every direction—dozens, hundreds, even thousands massing at the best dens. They bask, separately, above ground on warm days, and slip beneath on cold days. On none of those days do they eat. They're emptying their guts of every particle of food. They must go into their winter confinement clean.

Since mid-November, frost has kept them in their underground cell, a chamber deeper than the four feet the frost will seep in the months to come. Pools of water and thick, humid air keep their skin supple. With no food in them to rot, they've stopped all digestion. Digestion burns energy. They've positioned themselves where the chamber stays between thirty-seven and thirty-nine degrees Fahrenheit, a temperature that slows the flow of energy through their bodies and holds them—perfectly poised—between life and death. They are conscious—conscious only to keep themselves as effortless as possible. To drink only when necessary. To move only if a hard winter's frost forces further descent.

The chill at the knife edge of death sparks a chain of changes in a small gland in the garter snake's brain. Beyond his knowing, he is being prepared. Then, when the ground above him warms, he's cued. The season for sparing himself is past. He and the multitude with him swim up through the dark layers of earth and break from the hole, falling onto each other, a writhing ball of snakes, mating. Nearly starved, they obey that more primal survival prod before hurrying off alone to hunt, spending all that they've saved, fervent for life to multiply, to abound.

Woodchuck

Knowing the complications below, I kneel in front of our garden shed and speak softly into the hole beneath its door: *Sleep well chuck.*

The hole plunges deeper than the frost line, then levels into a tunnel maybe as long as a three-story building is tall. At its end he's tucked, head between his hind paws, in a room padded with grass and leaves. He might hear me—his ears are that sharp—if he's awake. Certainly not if he's asleep. Even if a predator could navigate that long tunnel and nab the sleeping woodchuck and shake him, drop him, bite him, the sleeper would sleep on, limp and insensible.

That's not the threat. Deep in his burrow he's safe from other mouths. It's his own hunger he has to escape. Winter has wiped bare his vegetarian table. He would starve if he stayed awake. Asleep—a sleep so deep his heart barely beats and his body cools to nearly the temperature of ice—he expends almost no energy. Only at a glacial pace does he burn the fat he added eating up to three pounds of greens and fruit each lush day of summer. In deep sleep his hunger is subdued; his substance shrinks, but is not consumed.

And yet, he might be awake now, in the lean heart of Advent.

Whenever he sleeps, a finely calibrated inner clock ticks on. In abundant seasons it wakes him and sends him back to sleep on a predictable twenty-four-hour cycle. Now it lets him sink four, five, seven days down into a sleep so deep it amounts to self-absence. This both preserves him and stresses him mightily. At metabolic bottom, where sleep meets death, cellular sludge builds up, careful molecular balances tip . . . till his clock alarm rings, pulling him up, awake enough to use his toilet chamber and re-tune his body chemistry.

His inner clockwork also suffers the stress of absolute sleep. While he's awake it recalibrates to ensure its alarm will wake him when his body chemistry turns precarious again in the next bout of sleep. Also, his clock and the clocks of all the area's chucks recalibrate to stay entrained to a larger rhythm. No matter how long or short their individual cycles of wakefulness and sleep, the whole community is synchronized to a cycle of the earth itself and readied for a small window of opportunity.

Mid-February, the male under my shed and all his fellows will be waked, and this time crawl out of their burrows into the still barren world, looking for the homes of females. They will enter and acquaint themselves, males and females, but not mate. The window is not yet.

Their clocks send them back to their separate burrows to sleep again until the season's final alarm signals, *Now*. Now is the time to mate, so that the kits-to-come will be weaned at just the moment when the world's green food becomes abundant, so that they have every possible hour to eat and add weight before they must sleep, so that they will be stout enough to survive all the wakings of next winter. Then one spring day these young chucks too will wake into the ephemeral window and pass on the elegant rhythm that sustains them all.

Striped Skunk

Because her eyesight is poor, and because I was downwind and standing as still as I could bear in the mosquito-thick morning at the edge of the woods, I was insubstantial as a spirit to her. What was substantial—and consequential—was the quick cricket in the leafmeal. She thrust her pink-tipped nose into the leaf litter, tossed it aside, and pounced.

The sun was already up that late October morning and she hadn't retreated to a hollow log or stump to sleep away the day. *She knows,* I thought, *she knows the snow and cold are coming. She's hunting overtime, urgent to get fat.*

Or maybe she was out late that morning because she'd ceded some of her night feeding time to the other urgency of October: nest readying. All the rest of the year she beds in the hubbub above ground, but in the cold, spare season her survival sense forces her to go deeper. During that autumn night she might have been scraping together leaves and grass, pushing them ahead of her down a woodchuck hole, then deftly making her bed. No matter if the chuck was there. Gentle as she is, she happily shares the den with him; and anyway, awake or asleep, he stays in his chamber at the den's far end, leaving the rest to her. And her sisters.

A quiet soul, she prefers to make her way through the world alone, or with her kits. But when winter begins nipping at her shoulder, she compromises. She may have scraped, pushed, and shaped a full bushel of leaves and grass into a nest precisely to her liking. But come late November she might leave that perfect bed empty and join three or five or nine other females in the nest one of them has made. What matters is not whose nest, but togetherness.

By now, Advent's center, the skunks that find themselves denned together are curled into a single ball of black fur, white stripes undulating through it. Most nights they rouse for a few minutes. A couple may go to the entrance hole and, if it's not sealed up with snow, poke pink noses out into the sharp air. But soon they're all re-balled, drifting up and down the ladder of sleep.

Fat skunks can stay on the upper rungs of that ladder. Thinner sisters must slide deeper down the ladder and stay there asleep longer, burning less fat, but stressing their systems. Thicker or thinner, each shares her heat with the others, so all in the ball save fat they would have had to burn if alone. Fat is the only food each one has underground; tucked into the huddle, what she has goes further. And not only to sustain her single life. The several new lives she wants to make when winter ends can only take hold and grow in her if she has enough of herself left.

So, solitary the rest of the year, here she folds herself into others. Ninety days, a hundred—winter howls on. As the body of each one shrinks, they wrap the ball of their slighter selves tighter and lean into the warmth that, together, they are.

Porcupine

Though the day's light is fading, there's no mistaking his trail through several inches of powdery new snow. His short scuffing strides, tail sashaying behind, leave an undulating tread that looks like a thick snake slithering through a trough. The trail stops at the base of a sizable beech. I tip my head back, and back, until my eyes find him at the top. Through binoculars I see his small intent face peering out from an all-body parka of fluffed fur.

By mid-summer he had begun growing that prodigious double-layered coat. The long white-fringed hairs and quills I see radiating out from his face and sides and back wick away sleet and snow, keeping his underfur dry. Soft, downy, thick against his skin, this underlayer holds his body heat in against the pull of the winter wind. Much of the night he'll rock in the high branches, as warm at his ninety-eight-degree core as I am in my bed.

He's not up there for the rocking ride. He's there for the food. Lips closed behind his four long orange incisors to seal his warm mouth from the cold, he scrapes the bark in repeating triangles, not missing an inch. He opens his lips long enough to shunt the woody fiber back to his grinding teeth. There's not much a body can make of bark. But his gut has adapted to eke from it every

available atom of nutrition. Those who've leaned into one say a porcupine in winter smells strongly of old sawdust.

Despite the marvels of his digestion, his winter wood diet will deplete him. All summer and fall he fattened himself on buds and leaves and nuts to protect against the loss. But other than growing a thicker coat around a thicker body, he takes none of the protective measures of his neighbors. He doesn't sleep deeply; he doesn't retreat underground or build a warm nest; he doesn't stash food or huddle with others. Rather, he exposes himself to winter's coldest place and time: the treetops at night.

Well before dawn the porcupine will inch his way in from the tree's crown and down the trunk, tail quills acting like crampons. After a night's work his stocky legs wade even more slowly through the snow. His trip home is short. Because snow travel so taxes his body, he has chosen his winter house shrewdly. The beech where he eats tonight is one in a stand of beech trees, with a few sugar maples, which he also eats, mixed among them. This is his winter pantry, and within two hundred yards of it, a hollow oak tree. A thick mat of droppings on the front stoop marks the oak as his own.

Inside, out of the wind but eschewing the comfort of a nest, he assumes the pose of his winter rest. Sitting up, he tucks the unfurred patch of his rump beneath him so it won't leak heat. He folds his forelimbs close to his thinly furred chest and turns in his broad back limbs to shield his thinly furred belly. Lone ascetic in the dim heart of the tree, he closes his eyes and hugs himself, warmed by his own radiant core.

Common Eastern Firefly

My neighbors have strung little white lights in their dogwood tree. The lights blink in a cheerful, if mechanical, way. They make me wish for the wild lights of summer that bobbed and dipped around that tree and across all the yards as far as we could see. A warmer yellow-green, the living lights punctuated the dark with bright periods and swooping exclamation points, finishing sentences we couldn't parse but which conveyed delight.

The fireflies of July and August died days after mesmerizing us. It was a mating dance that lit them up, and with their eggs fertilized and planted in the earth, the purpose of their brief and shining adult life was accomplished.

But their light didn't die. Underground, when tapped or bumped by a passing insect or mole, the eggs would answer with a faint glow. After about two weeks, transparent red-eyed larvae broke from the eggs. Miniscule and wormlike, with six legs and two antennae, they have, since the moment they emerged, radiated a soft and constant light.

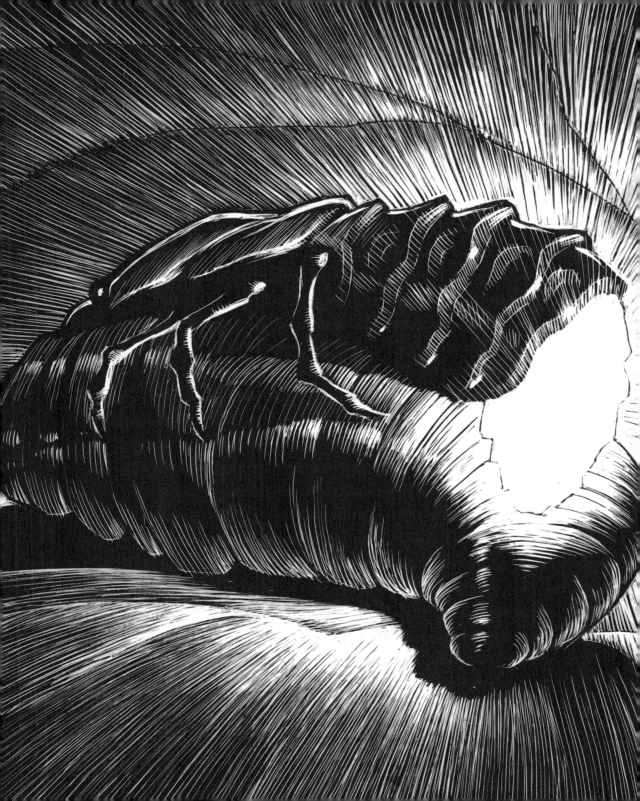

Standing beside the blinking dogwood tree in December I think of them, far beneath my feet, glowing still. They're crawling through the dark soil at night here. The size of small crumbs when they were hatched, they came equipped with toxins in their mouths which make them mighty, enabling them to paralyze, dissolve, and drink soft-bodied creatures many times their size, like earthworms.

As they eat, the larvae outgrow themselves—repeatedly. Pinched in their own skin, they slough it off and grow another. Soon that skin confines and has to go. It takes some time for the new self-covering to set. Left soft and naked, still they shine, their low glow warning predators that to eat them would be a fatal mistake.

For almost a year firefly larvae live this secret life, unseen and utterly unlike the creatures they will be. Later this winter, frost will force them to go deeper underground. But at every level their purpose is the same: to eat and grow, eat and grow. Here in mid-December, about halfway through their wormlike existence, they are still and only intent on enlargement. By late spring each will have grown to half the length of one of the little lights strung in the dogwood tree.

When it senses it has grown fully, a larva will construct a sort of mud cave for itself in the soil. It will lie in the cave, glowing and still, while every part of its body melts and is remade. It will have crawled through the dark earth for more than three hundred days to be made ready for a transformation that happens in ten or twelve. A new creature, nothing like a worm, will push out of its cave, dig, and break above ground. It will rest a moment and breathe, then rise on fresh wings, its light, long hidden, released to dance through the wide nights of summertime.

Meadow Vole

Our path to the woods cuts through a field of tall grasses, goldenrod, asters, and thistles, all brown and brittle now, crowned with snow. Ahead of me, my dog suddenly stops. She leans forward, staring at the patch of snow where next she would have stepped. Then she pitches herself into it, an inelegant half dive, muzzle rooting through the powder to get to ground. Also sharp-eared, the meadow voles heard her first and, again, escaped.

On the surface the field's snow is broken only by our footfalls. Beneath, it's tunneled in a labyrinth of runways leading to and from nests, communal toilet areas, and feeding sites. In winter the voles seldom surface from the tunnels that hide them from predators and insulate them from the harshest weather. Under a silent white roof a whole society hurries along.

Hurry it must. The heft of fifteen pennies in your palm, an adult meadow vole each day must eat as much as she weighs. That imperative pushes her to go looking for food about every three hours, around the clock. In winter her food is more scarce and she burns more energy trying to stay warm while searching for it. Responding to this scarcity and cold, a meadow vole makes what seems

a death wish. In summer, when her favorite green plants grow profligately, she does not busy herself packing on body fat, nor does she stockpile seeds near her nest. Not only does she eschew accumulation, she now goes a step further: she sheds weight for winter. Thinner, she loses body heat more quickly at the very coldest time of year.

Counterintuitive though it is, going lighter is the lynchpin of her survival strategy. Lighter, she needs less food. Though she still goes out every three hours, she comes back sooner. She needs fewer minutes each trip to find enough seeds, bark, and blanched grass stems to sustain her. Those are minutes the vole can spend resting in her nest of woven grass, where the temperature can be a cozy fifty degrees Fahrenheit. There she saves the energy her heavier self would have used up, running the tunnels to find enough food; and, insulated in her cup of warmth, she saves herself from the strain of generating all her own heat.

Her pared-down self is even the reason the nest is so warm. In all other seasons she mates continuously and allows only her tiny pups to lie with her. Now the shorter, darker days have shut off the tap of her reproductive hormones. Missing them is part of the reason her body mass shrinks and easily loses heat. But without those fierce mating and maternal juices, she gentles; she's willing to welcome neighbors, kin or not, into her nest. Then, when each, alone, is smallest, most vulnerable to the cold, they huddle together, peaceable creatures whose communion creates the heat that shelters them all.

Eastern Fox Squirrel

The sun is not quite up, but the six fox squirrels at home in my backyard have roused from their nests and dash along the latticework of branches as I walk across the snow. They know what's in my bag. Before I can put a handful of raw peanuts on the feeder, the boldest one runs down the trunk of the hickory tree. He stops, stretches and yawns, then takes in his mouth the peanut I offer.

What I bring are treats, not sustenance. Each fox squirrel needs about two pounds of nuts every week to keep running and leaping all winter long. It's a high-energy lifestyle they lead, regardless of the season, and they do count its cost. They have an investment plan, a plan that's all about food.

The squirrel pack quickly consumes my offerings. Then the bold male hops through the snow, stops abruptly, and plunges groundward, waving the flag of his tail. When he pops up, his mouth is bulged wide with an acorn. He knew it was there. He knew it was a red oak acorn, a rich energy gem. He buried it himself after a fall day's feeding spree.

Perched in the hickory and oak trees, he and his companions would speed eat—dropping nuts only partially consumed—working to add as much fat as possible, and as quickly as possible, in order to spend time on their main investment strategy. Glutted, the squirrels ran to the ground and scattered, burying nuts hauled from the trees. Each squirrel burying one nut at a time, time after time—it seemed a huge spill of energy. But it would have cost them more energy still—and been futile—to fend off the deer, turkeys, and raccoons that also crave the fat-dense nutmeats. Instead, the squirrels hid them, to keep for themselves the food that fuels their winter liveliness.

Not white oak acorns, though. Most of these they ate on the spot. Whites, they know, sprout within days, rendering them useless as food. But red oak acorns they wisely—and shrewdly—buried. Less tasty, yes, but reds stay unsprouted in the cold ground. Plus, they deliver a more powerful dose of energy, badly needed in the bleakest cold. These the squirrels took greater pains to protect, hiding them farther from the tree so thieves will be less likely to uncover them.

Including thieves of their own kind, always nearby and watching. Thus, my favorite male employed a bag of nut-burying tricks. He would dig a decoy hole—or two, or more—before depositing a nut. Or after. He came back later and reburied nuts in new places. Some of his stashes will be found, even under a carpet of snow, by the keen noses of his neighbors. And he will find some of theirs. Those are bonuses. What he depends on to survive the barren season is the power of memory.

I imagine him curled in his nest, a wind-tight ark of leaves and twigs high in the tree, each night consulting the map in his memory. On it is impressed not only the location of each nut, but also its kind. Which of the thousand shall he retrieve tomorrow, which shall he save for a colder day? Winter relentlessly tests the spirited life he leads. He does his utmost to answer, remembering one small buried treasure after another.

Red Fox

The longest night of the year retreats reluctantly. Slow to wake, morning seeps in, gray and grainy. Startling, then, the quick orange brush stroked against the snow at the field's edge—her signature curving into the thicket and gone.

Finally the fox will rest. It's likely she's been out since the sun set yesterday, fifteen dark hours ago, hours keenly focused on quieting her hunger. The berries and autumn fruits she loves are gone. The beetles, other insects, and lizards—perished or burrowed underground. Most birds—far flown. And few creatures have died from exposure this early into winter, or she would feed her urgent body with their fallen ones.

I turn my route toward her vanishing point. Intersecting her tracks I follow and see them change—they fall closer together and pivot a quarter turn, then stop. For six feet or so the snow lies quiet, unbroken. Then a churned commotion of a hole, and two drops of blood.

Minutes ago the fox was trotting westward across the field when tiny rustling, shuffling, squeaking sounds rippled through the snow from as far away

as a football field and into the soft receptacles of her ears. She stopped. She cocked her head side to side—right ear high, left ear high—measuring the split-second lag between the rustle-squeak reaching one ear, then the other. Thus she estimated where under the white expanse its source stirred. But to stay alive she needs precision.

Once she'd taken the sound's measure, she crept ahead, ears alert, furred pillows of her paws falling with less than a whisper on the snow. Then, still listening, she turned, aiming her body-of-attention just east of true north. She saw north. It seems Earth's magnetic field creates a patch of shadow on her eye's retina to show her north. When she turned north, the shadow she saw went ahead of her, step by deliberate step. Homing in, she lined up the shadow—always the same, precise distance from her—with the shifting, under-snow sound.

For a breath she crouched. Then she reared onto her hind legs, knees bent, launching up and out on a trajectory into which she had factored speed and direction of the invisible scurrying, depth and resistance of the snow cover. In mid-air she made minute corrections with the rudder of her tail. At the peak of a precisely ordered arc, she plunged. For a silent instant she seemed headless in the snow. Then she wriggled up out of the crater she'd made. Righted, she lifted her muzzle skyward and gulped.

Though she listens intently to detect the distant wisp of sound, though she trains on it the whole of her attention, allowing no distractions as she moves in with steps polished into silence, in winter these remarkable powers are insufficient. To complete them, to find the hidden nourishment, she must turn in the direction of the shadow. If she leaps without its reliable lead, she will come up empty four out of five times. Following it, she is fed.

Northern Cardinal

Iron-gray clouds weight the pond and field. Beyond them the thicket and naked trees endure the day. Heavy, my head bows. I watch my boots trudge. Then my head snaps up and left, my eye snagged and carried by a scarlet flame lilting through the tall weeds till it lights, setting a-sway the leggy skeleton of a thistle, and rides.

When nearly all the world tamps down its color, this male cardinal flares—an extravagant gesture considering the hawk, whose dark eye snaps to him faster than mine. His brilliance shouts his unshakeable expectation of spring. In spring he will court. The redder his plumage, the more ardently females will fly to him. So in the fall, when growing the feathers he'll wear in courting season, he fed himself almost exclusively fruits like dogwood berries, wild grapes, and multiflora rose hips—fruits that saturate him in scarlet.

Extravagant, yes, but not reckless. To bring his flame through months of cold that strip the world to the bone, he must give deep attention to his body. The flight that caught my eye and heart was no joyride. Swaying on the thistle stalk, he did not sing. Not in winter. Flying, singing—these burn energy, use him

up. Clothed in the color of passionate abandon, he is in truth a conserver, asking of every action, *Does it have a purpose? Does it repay what it costs?*

To fuel his life, winter leaves him only seeds. As the cold sharpens he needs more seeds to fuel his furnace to its 105-degree Fahrenheit survival heat—just when other seed eaters also need more and snow is apt to cover the uneaten seeds. So in late fall and early winter, he chooses to eat more than he needs—but exactingly. He knows he soon must wear a reserve of fat or he'll freeze. Too little fat, and he will fall. But too much fat, and he will also fall. Fat slows him, fat slurs his dart and weave. And the hawk, watching the open fields of weed and grain, watching the backyard feeders, dives quick and clean.

So each day the cardinal weighs his reserve. He senses precisely how much fat is spread beneath his thin skin. Also, he takes a measure of the temperature and length of day, sensing how much winter remains. He places all he knows in a finely felt balance, which tells him how much he must eat to add an exact increment of fat. By fractions of grams he grows himself so that he is weightiest exactly when winter is most harsh and food meager. He aims for a scalpel's edge: just heavy enough each week of intensifying cold to fuel his purposes, just light enough to whisk away should talons fall from the sky.

The cardinal holds on as the thistle slows its sway. Maybe he's weighing himself, noting how far the stalk dipped when he landed, how fast it bounds back. If he can navigate the narrow path between too thick and too thin, too much and too little, he'll arrive at his long-expected spring. He'll blaze out then, and dazzle—bobbing, flitting, cavorting, singing *what-cheer, what-cheer, what-cheer.*

Lake Trout

Eight hundred feet out on a pier in northern Lake Michigan I wince against the sleet and spray stinging my face. Every Christmas Eve I come back here; it's the place I first called home. Still, the surging gray tonnage bashing headlong against the breakwater, against the long-suffering shore, rattles me to the bone.

Somewhere below the uproar glides a silver fish speckled in ivory. She welcomes the tumultuous waves, and the cold. Tumult and cold mix more oxygen into the water, and cold, oxygen-rich water brought lake trout here in the wake of receding glaciers. Rich breathing is better to her than any particular food. Though she will swim the three-hundred-mile length of this Great Lake looking for the small fish she prefers, if she doesn't find enough of them, she'll simply switch to tiny shrimp or insects. And if these go missing, she'll choose to be vegetarian, consenting thereby to grow more slowly. Darwin, and other scientists since, have thought her species to be perhaps the most flexible, most adaptive vertebrate on earth.

Now, in early winter, she's at her ease. In other seasons she will sometimes follow small fish into water warmer than her internal organs like, choosing to

bear this stress for the sake of the food that satisfies her best. Or she may spare herself the stress and eat less nutritious fare. Always she's aware of the tradeoff and of having to choose. But in winter the warmer water—which the small fish follow—is not much more than forty degrees Fahrenheit, a temperature just right for her body. Bathed in comfort, with ample food besides, she can relax.

She relaxes alone. Seven or eight weeks ago she lived her communal life. It lasted a few days. In late fall, when she felt the water cool, an irrepressible urge rose in her and lake trout everywhere to return to their first homes—the beds where they hatched. Half of the hatching beds in Lake Michigan are straight out from this pier. It's not temperature or depth or clarity that make these waters so hospitable a first home. It's not the food supply. It's the rocks—limestone cobbles the size of doorknobs and soup bowls heaped six or more feet thick, some on shoals, some at the bottom of deep trenches. From all ends of the lake the fish massed here. Through the night males and females swam over the great rock piles where they had first come awake, silver sides pressed together.

When the female swam away and resumed her solitary lake wandering, she left behind thousands of fertile eggs, fallen from her body into crevices between the cobbles. It's a kind of faith this shining fish practices, returning, perhaps from a vast distance, to plant life in the place where she came to life. It's faith in the goodness of the rocks, their sheltering crannies, their cold-water cradles. She tucked her eggs there, away from predators, away from churning currents. Then she left. She's done all she can do. Vital but dormant, the eggs wait, as she once waited, until winter ends. It's what they must do to wake.

Jesus, the Christ

On our way to the woods my dog veered left, off the path. I've learned that following her, on days I'm awake, leads to revelation. She brought me to a small manger made of new wood freshly sawed and nailed together. Made in the traditional Nativity-scene shape, the manger had been placed at the edge of the woods. It was empty.

I suspected the four children living in the house nearby. Outdoors often, aided by their parents, they play games in the woods involving lightsabers, capes, and crowns. They are still seers.

The manger appeared a week into Advent. Brittle brown leaves from the oak above blew into and out of it. Then one day the manger was not empty. It was filled to the brim with hay. Two days later the hay had been dumped onto the ground and the manger moved a few feet away. It was now half full of shelled corn. A single fox squirrel sat up in the manger, leisurely eating kernel after kernel.

I found the children pulling each other through the snow on sleds. "Tell me about the manger," I said.

The oldest, a boy, said, "It's for the deer. We like to watch them. Next we're going to put a hunk of salt. . . ."

"It's for *all* the animals," interrupted the smallest, a girl, who had her head tipped back, mouth open to taste the falling flakes.

In the fullness of time, the Christmas story says, a girl gave birth ringed by animals. She lay the baby in one of their feeding troughs, where animal bodies would warm the air around his fresh-born human body. Mother and child fell asleep and woke to their chuffs and shuffling hooves, their calls and the shuddering of their hides. Later sheep herders smelling of dirt, damp wool, and milk crowded into the stable. Out in the wild night fields these animal men sitting in the dark were the first to get the word. A baby had been born, they were told, who would show people a way out of their small pinched lives, a way to abandon themselves to the ever-present, unstoppable current of Love that carries all things to radiant wholeness. To recognize him they should look for a child at home among animals.

At the edge of the woods where children put out corn and salt and watch for them, and name them and speak to them, the animals wait. Will they one day find the manger empty, the children indoors? So much rushes children into dropping their capes and crowns in the leafmeal; so much clamors and flashes for their attention. As they grow, will they lose the sight that sees light and spirit in other creatures? Or will they, despite the rush and clamor, find irresistible the beauty quietly radiating from everything that is? To the animals it makes all the difference. Their hope, and the hope of all that breathes, is that human ones abandon themselves to the One Great Love. For that, all creation waits.

ACKNOWLEDGMENTS

It was, first, humbling, and then heartwarming to realize how much help I needed to write this small book, including the help of people I will never know.

Thank you to all of the close observers of animals—scientists and self-trained animal watchers—who have written books, articles, and blogs on the ways of the creatures in this book, or who offered me their knowledge in emails, phone calls, and in-person conversations. This includes my dad.

Thank you to my two close readers: Tamara Dean, who embodies in a beautiful tension the sensibilities of both artist and scientist; and Cheryl Hellner, who unfailingly reminded me to look and listen deeply to the animals, and then again, more deeply.

Thank you to The Diamond Sisters, the small group of women artists who prayed me through this book.

Thank you to David Klein for his partnership in bringing the animals to life on the page. Thank you, too, to my editor at Paraclete Press, Phil Fox Rose, for honoring me as an artist.

Thank you to my sons, Kai and Cotter, whose love and wonder led me to make our family's animal Advent calendar, which led, twenty years later, to this book.

Finally, thank you Doug, for giving me space and time without ever asking what good I was making of it.

ABOUT PARACLETE PRESS

Who We Are

As the publishing arm of the Community of Jesus, Paraclete Press presents a full expression of Christian belief and practice—from Catholic to Evangelical, from Protestant to Orthodox, reflecting the ecumenical charism of the Community and its dedication to sacred music, the fine arts, and the written word. We publish books, recordings, sheet music, and video/DVDs that nourish the vibrant life of the church and its people.

What We Are Doing

BOOKS | PARACLETE PRESS BOOKS show the richness and depth of what it means to be Christian. While Benedictine spirituality is at the heart of who we are and all that we do, our books reflect the Christian experience across many cultures, time periods, and houses of worship.

We have many series, including *Paraclete Essentials*; *Paraclete Fiction*; *Paraclete Poetry*; *Paraclete Giants*; and for children and adults, *All God's Creatures*, books about animals and faith; and San Damiano Books, focusing on Franciscan spirituality. Others include *Voices from the Monastery* (men and women monastics writing about living a spiritual life today), *Active Prayer*, and new for young readers: *The Pope's Cat*. We also specialize in gift books for children on the occasions of Baptism and First Communion, as well as other important times in a child's life, and books that bring creativity and liveliness to any adult spiritual life.

The MOUNT TABOR BOOKS series focuses on the arts and literature as well as liturgical worship and spirituality; it was created in conjunction with the Mount Tabor Ecumenical Centre for Art and Spirituality in Barga, Italy.

MUSIC | The Paraclete Recordings label represents the internationally acclaimed choir *Gloriæ Dei Cantores*, the *Gloriæ Dei Cantores Schola*, and the other instrumental artists of the *Arts Empowering Life Foundation*.

Paraclete Press is the exclusive North American distributor for the Gregorian chant recordings from St. Peter's Abbey in Solesmes, France. Paraclete also carries all of the Solesmes chant publications for Mass and the Divine Office, as well as their academic research publications.

In addition, Paraclete Press Sheet Music publishes the work of today's finest composers of sacred choral music, annually reviewing over 1,000 works and releasing between 40 and 60 works for both choir and organ.

VIDEO | Our video/DVDs offer spiritual help, healing, and biblical guidance for a broad range of life issues including grief and loss, marriage, forgiveness, facing death, understanding suicide, bullying, addictions, Alzheimer's, and Christian formation.

Learn more about us at our website:
www.paracletepress.com or
phone us toll-free at 1.800.451.5006

SCAN
TO
READ
MORE

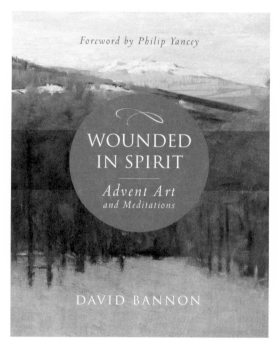

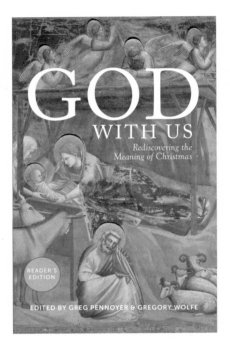
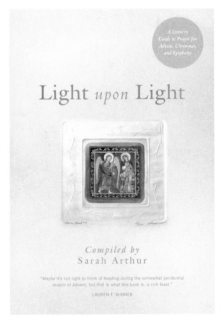